START-UP
SCIENCE

LIGHT AND DARK

Claire Llewellyn

Evans

Published by Evans Brothers Limited
2A Portman Mansions
Chiltern Street
London W1U 6NR

Reprinted 2006

Produced for Evans Brothers Limited by
White-Thomson Publishing Ltd.
2/3 St Andrew's Place
Lewes, East Sussex BN7 1UP

Printed in China by WKT Company Limited

Editor: Dereen Taylor
Consultants: Les Jones, Science Consultant, Manchester
Education Partnership; Norah Granger, former primary
headteacher and senior lecturer in education, University
of Brighton
Designer: Leishman Design

Cover (centre): Chris Fairclough Colour Library
Cover (top left, top right): Chris Fairclough

British Library Cataloguing in Publication Data
Llewellyn, Claire
    Light and dark - (Start-up science)
    1.Ligh - Juvenile literature
    I.Title
    535

ISBN: 0 237 52591 7
13-digit ISBN (from 1 Jan 2007) 978 0 237 52591 0

Acknowledgements:
Special thanks to the following for their help and
involvement in the preparation of this book: Staff and
pupils at Elm Grove Primary School, Brighton, Liz Price
and family and friends.

Picture Acknowledgements:
Corbis 4, 5, 12, 13, 16, 20 (right); Chris Fairclough
Colour Library 6, 9 (bottom), 14, 19 (bottom); Ecoscene
7 (right); Eye Ubiquitous 7 (left), 21 (right); Popperfoto 8
(left), 19 (top); Sally & Richard Greenhill 17 (top); Zul
Mukhida 21 (left); All other photographs by Chris
Fairclough.

Contents

Bright Sun, dull cloud

The Sun is shining and the air is warm. The sea is blue and sparkling. It's the perfect day to go to the beach.

► Look at this picture of a beach.
How can you tell that the Sun is very bright?

⚡WARNING!

Never look directly at the Sun, even through sunglasses. It could burn your eyes.

Every morning the Sun rises and the sky grows light. On some days, the sky is full of clouds. They block the Sun's bright light.

▼ Look at this picture of the beach. What changes do you notice on a cloudy day?

Sunny days or cloudy days – which do you prefer?

rises   light   clouds   cloudy   sunny   **5**

The end of the day

Every evening, the Sun sets and the sky gets dark.
Minute by minute, the light begins to fade.
We see things less clearly now.

Seeing is one of our body's senses.

evening   sets   dark   fade   seeing

Many animals can see better at night than we can. Some animals use their sense of smell or hearing to find their way in the dark.

▼ Can you match these two animals to the descriptions below?

This animal's eyes are big and shiny.
This animal sniffs out slugs and worms.

senses   smell   hearing   shiny

Turn on the lights

When it gets dark outside, we turn on electric lights. They help us to see.

lamplight floodlights torchlight traffic lights

▼ Look at the lights in these four pictures. Can you match them to the words above?

electric lamplight floodlights

Which are the **brightest** lights? Can you think of any other places where we use lights at night?

▼ What other lights can you see in the picture below?

torchlight   traffic lights   brightest   9

Candlelight

It is Olivia's birthday. Mum has lit the candles on her cake. The candles give out light. Candlelight shows up well in the dark.

lit candles candlelight brighter

▼ Candlelight is not like electric light. Which one is brighter and better to see by? When else might you use candlelight?

▼ A lit match also gives out light. When the flame is tall, the light is bright. What happens as the flame dies down?

⚡WARNING!
Fire is dangerous.
Never play with fire.

match   flame   fire   dangerous

Dark places

In some places, like tunnels and mines, there is never any sunlight. These places are deep underground. The Sun's light cannot reach them.

▲ Do you know where these dark places are? What is helping these people to see?

tunnels   mines

▼ **Moles live in underground burrows where it is always dark. They use their long snout and whiskers to find their way around.**

How do you find your way around in the dark?
How does the dark make you feel?

deep   underground

Does it reflect light?

It can be dangerous on the roads at night. Drivers cannot see people clearly.

◄ This paramedic is wearing a jacket with shiny stripes. It reflects car headlights and helps her to be seen. This helps to keep her safe on the road.

clearly   reflects   headlights   safe

Other things around us reflect light. Most of them, like this ball, are shiny. The ball sparkles in the light. It doesn't give out light itself. You wouldn't be able to see it in the dark.

Look for shiny things that reflect light in your home. How many can you find?

sparkles

Warning lights

Bright lights are easy to see. They help to get our attention. Some bright lights warn us of danger.

▶ This light warns sailors to keep away from these rocks.

attention warn danger

Look at the
lights in these
pictures.

What are they
warning us
about?

Light and dark words

There are many different words to describe light and dark. These are some of the words that we could use to describe this dark wood:

shadowy   dim   gloomy   shady

describe

sparkle twinkle

gleam glow

Look at the words
on this page.

flashing dazzling

blazing

Which ones best
describe the
lights in these
two pictures?

19

Festivals of light

Midwinter days are short and often gloomy. The nights are dark and cold. We enjoy festivals at this time. Some festivals have special lights that shine brightly in the dark.

midwinter festivals Christmas

Look at the lights in these four pictures. Can you match them to the correct festival?

Christmas Hanukkah Divali Bonfire Night

Hanukkah   Divali   Bonfire Night

Further information for

New words listed in the text:

attention	clearly	Divali	Hanukkah	mines	shiny	
Bonfire Night	clouds	electric	headlights	reflects	smell	tunnels
bright	cloudy	evening	hearing	rises	sparkles	underground
brighter	danger	fade	lamplight	safe	sparkling	warn
brightest	dangerous	festivals	light	seeing	Sun	
candlelight	dark	fire	lit	senses	sunny	
candles	deep	flame	match	sets	torchlight	
Christmas	describe	floodlights	midwinter	shining	traffic lights	

Possible Activities

PAGES 4-5

Take children into a park or playground on a day when there is sunshine and clouds. Without looking up at the sky, can they tell when the Sun goes behind a cloud or comes out again? How?

Discuss the importance of sun protection and the need for sun cream and sunhats. Explain that we should seek shade in the middle of a summer's day.

PAGES 6-7

Ask the children to make day/night pictures, showing what can be seen in the day and in the night.

Read poems or stories about night-time animals.

PAGES 8-9

Look for all the different electric lights in the classroom or at home.

Take children to the lighting department of a local store or make a collage of pictures showing many different electric lights.

Bring a table lamp into the classroom and explore all its different parts.

PAGES 10-11

Take children into a room that can be blacked out. Can they block out every bit of light so that the room is really dark?

Discuss fire safety with the children. Explain the risks of using candles and how these can be avoided.

PAGES 12-13

Discuss children's experiences of being in the dark. How do they feel when they are blindfolded?

Construct a black box with a tiny peephole at one end and a larger hole covered with cardbord in the top. Investigate how easy or hard it is to see things inside the box when the larger hole is partly or totally covered. Try using torches as well.

Parents and Teachers

PAGES 14-15

Talk about road safety and the importance of being seen in the evening and at night. What can children wear or carry to make themselves stand out?

Investigate reflective strips and other shiny surfaces. How and where would the children expect them to shine? Try out the children's ideas to find out if they were right.

PAGES 16-17

Make a list of all the vehicles that have flashing warning lights. How else do these vehicles warn people of danger?

Are there any machines in the classroom or at home that have warning lights? When do these come on?

PAGES 18-19

Collect pictures that could be the starting point for literacy work about light and dark (e.g. a gloomy forest, the night sky, a fairground). Make a list of words to suit each picture. Can children guess the picture from the words?

PAGES 20-21

Talk about special festivals. At what time of year do these festivals occur? When do people use the special lights?

Draw or paint a picture of a festival showing the special lights.

Further Information

BOOKS FOR CHILDREN

Little Bees: Rise and Shine A First Look at Light by Sam Godwin (Hodder Wayland, 2002)

The Christmas Story by Anita Ganeri (Evans Books, 2002)

The Divali Story by Anita Ganeri (Evans Books, 2002)

Toppers: Living with Light by Nicola Baxter (Franklin Watts, 2001)

Ways into Science: Light and Dark by Peter Riley (Franklin Watts, 2000)

World of Festivals: Hanukkah by Anne Clark, Gill Rose and David Rose (Evans Books, 1999)

BOOKS FOR ADULTS

How to Sparkle at Science Investigations by Monica Huns (Brilliant Publications)

WEBSITES

www.educate.org.uk

www.primaryresources.co.uk/science

Index